honor yourself

honor yourself
...an offering for those
lost in dark places

- terri st.cloud

bone sigh books

ISBN: 978-0-9815440-0-7 (pbk)
bone sigh arts
www.bonesigharts.com
www.bonesighbooks.com

cover art: yohan
www.bfg-productions.com

book layout / design:
zakk and yo
www.mazuzu.com

contents

contents

i started out wanting to dedicate this book
to someone i lost. someone WE lost. someone
precious who couldn't find her way out of the darkness.
this book was born because of her, and i wanted
it to be her book.

and then i watched, and i listened, and it grew.
the dedication grew to include you.
because while this book was born thru someone else,
it's here because of you. with the hope that it might
help you find the awareness that you aren't alone.
that there is light in the darkness.
i wanted it to be your book.

and then, because i can't do anything the easy way,
it grew some more,
it grew into wanting to honor something inside me.
something i have trouble holding onto, but when i
do hold it, it changes everything.
trust.
i wanted to honor trust in the universe.
i wanted it to be the universe's book.

altho i knew....it already was...

to the universe...

to you...

to someone very precious to me...

i dedicate this book.

Sometimes in the darkest dark, we think we're all alone. we think that no one could possibly know. that no one could possibly care, understand, feel, or share any of the feelings we are having. that's just not true. those thoughts are mistaken. it is then that we need to turn to someone who is there. someone who knows and understands. if you can't find them in person, find them in a book.

crawl if you can't walk. claw your way there if you have to. and when you get there, stay until you know that you aren't alone.

stay there and gather some strength. there is something you need to do. stay and start searching. there's something you have got to find. you have got to find your value. you have got to find your worth. you have got to know that you matter.

how? how do you find that when you're so far lost? maybe you're so lost, you're doing things to hurt yourself just to transfer some of the pain. you're so lost that you're sure you're worth nothing, and that if anyone could ever really see who you are, they'd agree. you are so lost and so hurting that you just want it to stop.

how do you get thru that?

you are not alone.

and the hurting can stop. maybe not as fast as you like....but it can and will stop. hold on tight to my hands. hold on as hard as you can. don't let go. i may not be standing right there with you physically, but i am right next to you in spirit. i've been thru my own darkness, and i've watched others thru theirs.

and right now, i am in the midst of grieving someone who didn't hang on. who couldn't find the right place for support, who didn't know the darkness would fade. who had no idea that she was a beautiful, talented, bright, shining being. she had no idea. no idea at all. i watch her family lost in grief, and i think of all that we're missing with her passing. i want to shout out to anyone feeling that they're worthless to stop. to rethink. to take your power back. to take the first step towards seeing your value.

take my hand and read these poems with me. they were birthed out of my own pain. they were birthed out of my own lack of seeing myself. they were birthed out of hardship....and they've taken me on a journey that I wouldn't trade for anything.

believing that i'd never fit in, and no one would ever understand me, i've come all the way around to believing that we all fit in and we all experience the same pain....and we are all connected. it's just different shades, different angles, different depths...but it's all there... all shared.

to find that connection, to start that journey, we have to find the part inside us that we are ignoring. the part that holds the beauty and is waiting patiently for us to come hold it too. it's up to us to go find it. it's up to us to reach out to touch it. it's up to us to take the journey.

it's okay that we don't know how.
it's just one step at a time.
bend that knee.
lift that foot.
and trust.

more than anything -

more than anything –
i want to trust a journey
that I don't understand.

forgiveness

she reached as deep as she could
inside her pain.
somewhere in there was a piece of
herself she needed to forgive.
and only then could her healing be complete.

playing it safe

the fear won't help save what you have -
it will make you lose what you could become.

the bear

you can try to feed the bear
but he will never get enough.
the best thing to do is feed yourself.

your truth

it is your truth.
your power.
your soul.
guard it with all you have.
don't let anyone's misconceptions steal it.
including your own

i will not run

i will accept the falls.
embrace my scars.
live my passion.
i will not run.

blue people

don't follow the blue people, she said.
they dull you and numb you...
travel down to your cave.
there you will discover your depths
and your heights.
and it is there you will gather the explosives to light
your life on fire.

birth

she was telling him about giving birth~
"one of the most amazing things about it is
you have to totally trust thru the worst pain.
all you can do is release control and trust."
she stopped and stared at him.
the tears came.
"i guess that's not just during birth,
is it?" she asked, reaching for his hand.

herself

she'd been fighting herself so long now,
the idea of trusting herself seemed foreign.
and yet...if she could trust...
if she could just trust herself ~
she just might discover the best
friend she's ever known.

time for real

it was when she casually mentioned
"fake happiness" that her world
stood still. she knew what she
meant all too well.
she had lived it.
become it.
it was time for real.
she wanted real happiness.
needed it.
deserved it.
demanded it.
took it!

her power

she took her power back ~
without permission.

forcing her

it was a gift they could never love her
entirely -
for then she was forced to do it
herself.

best parts

she let go of the shame
and the guilt,
seeing that she couldn't have
become who she was
without those past mistakes.
it was time to
honor them
and thank them,
and know that they were
some of the best parts
of her.

living passion

it is not enough to find your passion...
you must dive straight into the fire of your fear~
where you can grab it and hold it
until it transforms you.

seeing

the power lie in the seeing.
until she could see herself
with her own eyes,
she would not regain her power.

her giant

she called upon the different parts of
herself for help.
if she was going to make it,
she needed to accept them all,
unite them all
and believe in them all.
it was time for a huddle of
tremendous proportions.
it was the making of her giant.

the whole

she could never go back and make some of
the details pretty. All she could do was move
forward and make the whole beautiful.

allowing it

it's not about controlling.
it's about being present,
being open
being aware –
and allowing it to come

a vow to my heart

i will work on the act of listening to you
and my listening abilities will grow.
i will honor those things you relay to me
and act upon them.
when i act upon them, i will know that
i am living my truth
and owe no explanations to anyone.
i will believe in your ability to accept all emotions
and will not close down to protect you.
i will direct my energies and my power
to places that will strengthen you, not deplete you.
i will follow you
in the way i wish the world would follow you.
the child of the universe and the heart shall meld
and we shall dance as one.

silver linings

i walked thru hell and burned my soul…
ashes falling from my hands…
part of me lost forever.
grieving,
i found the others,
burnt and charred like me.
holding on to each other,
i knew –
even hell had a silver lining.

mantra

i will not allow myself to
be less than I am
to meet anybody's
expectations.

perhaps

perhaps power is letting go of the grip of the past
and standing empty handed facing the
future.

continuing on

almost crumbling to the ground, she stopped.
looking at how far she had traveled and all it had
taken to get there, she recognized her strength.
the strengths she had inside of her,
the strength she had gained along the way ~
her inner power.
and so, she stood up.
standing tall, she faced forward and continued on.

behind the fire

she sat back and trembled.
it was time to face another fear.
and yet, it really wasn't another fear~
they were all parts of one big huge one,
weren't they?
it was too late to stop now.
she could see who she was behind the fire ~
and she was heading straight for her.

fitting in

it saddened her at first.
she didn't fit in.
she had never fit in.
she didn't think she ever would.
but then, slowly, the smile came...
and grew.
she fit in with herself now.
for the first time she had grown
into herself and fit.
and that was enough.

her beauty

i look at her and see beauty,
and yet, she's been told she's not beautiful.
i watch her and see love,
and yet, she's been told she's not lovely.
i want to shout to her
"you are precious beyond words!"
yet i know she can't hear me.
and so i won't shout.
i will just keep believing in her
and reminding her.
and wait for her to see it,
to hear it,
and to know it
as deeply as i do.

in

she was scared again.
seems she was scared a lot these days.
time for a deep breath
and another plunge in.
it was the only way to get to
where she wanted to go.
so, in she went.

faded jeans

that difficult relationship had been on her mind
as she gazed at her old jeans in her closet.
she had loved those jeans so much.
never wanting to admit that she had outgrown them.
that they didn't fit her anymore.
they had given her a sense of comfort and
security for so long.
until holes came.
patches didn't hold up like she had hoped.
too tight around her now.
uncomfortable.
hurting her.
suddenly she knew ~
the time had come to let them go.

pieces of her heart

there were pieces of her heart
lying around cold and lonely.
unhonored.
gradually she gathered them together.
taking her heart back,
she made it hers again.

she became real

from her sorrow she found compassion.
from her grief she learned understanding.

and from her journey she became real.

voices

the pull was calling again.
so strongly it called her.
no.
she didn't want to answer it...
and yet....
she stalled. give it enough time.
it will pass. "stall." she told herself.
"you can do it."
the voices in her head going back and forth,
the struggle intense, the moments magnified.
and then slowly the call weakened.
the spirit strengthened.
she stepped forward with relief and pride.
she was moving on ~
with an even stronger spirit and a stronger body.

her light

anger boiled inside of her,
strong and furious.
reasons to lash out ran thru her head.
arguments not to countered them.
tension, frustration and tears filled her.
and then the words came...
"my soul is my own."
suddenly the target of her anger
lost its power.
she would give it no more.
she turned away
and moved towards her Light.

the veil

the veil is no longer needed.
drop it and see.
and know the beauty that is you.

the Light

finding the crack of light,
she pried her fingers in its edges.
pulling the darkness back
with all her strength,
the ocean of light poured forth.
weeping tears of gratitude,
she felt the Light flood over her.

come here

seems she always ran when
things got tough.
ran the other way.
ran and hid.
ran.
not this time.
she stood straight up,
took a deep breath
and said
"come here."

trials

"these trials, you know,"
she said,
"these rough spots,
they are making you into who
you want to become.
you do know that, don't you?"
she asked as she wiped my tears.
and now I really did know.

history in her veins

at times she called it baggage,
dragging its heavy weight along.
other times she called it fuel,
using it to push her forward.
now she called it
history in her veins
and just accepted it as part of
her life flow.

grace

maybe grace is figuring out it's not
all about you.
that people are doing what they're
doing for their own reasons.
not yours.
and maybe grace is accepting that.

she valued

and she valued herself.

somehow

"it's entirely up to me," she thought.
terror filled her.
but she'd do it anyway.
because somehow she could.

undercurrents

scratch the surface of her joy and you will find a
well of sorrow.
dive into the well and discover her spring of hope.
follow that spring to the river of her strength,
compassion and faith...
immerse yourself in her river
and you will have touched her soul.

unearthed

shovel full after shovel full,
she unearthed her self.
kneeling at the beauty
that had been buried,
she cleansed it with her tears
and lifted her self
into the Light.

training

their eyes had trained a life time
of looking past her.
and she had gotten her training
from them.
it was time to look at herself,
see the pain,
hold the ache

and love the girl inside.

she kept going

she began to see the swirl of opposites inside her –
searing pain and tremendous love included.
focusing on the love and allowing the pain,
she kept going

weaving

in and out
up and down
over and over
she wove the strands of her life together.
patching hole after hole
eventually she saw it was more than
the threads that gave her strength,
it was in the very act of weaving itself,
that she became strong.

kai's blessing

may you know the fire within you.
may you never doubt your connection to it.
may you learn the balance of holding it close and giving it freely.
and may you dance with the light that you shine.

making space

it is the act of allowing good things to come
that lives are transformed.

nope.

they were wrong.
she was okay just the way she was.

commitment

it is in the commitment to trust
that mountains begin to move.
it is in the commitment to love,
that walls begin to crumble,
and it is in the commitment to one's self
that worlds unimagined begin to become
real.

the thaw

there was a time the ice had saved her -
now only the thaw could.

honoring them

she wept
and she ached
and she held her head.
they had died because
they had never been seen.
she felt an iron determination creep over her.
it was time to see herself -
and honor them.

travels

"do you really think i can do it?" he asked.
"there are no limits," she said.
"none.
when you truly trust - deep down
'you trust no matter what' trust,
the limits fade away
and you travel to unknown places.
there's just one thing you need to decide.
do you really want to travel?"

her cathedral

she kneeled at the cave entrance -
hands had quietly removed
the snow and ice that had blocked her view.
lit in warmth and sacredness
she gazed upon her cathedral.

stepping up

yeah, she'd step up to the plate.
let the universe throw what it would.
she was in for the game.....
and she would not sit on the bench.

fabric of the universe

you, my child, are not
throw away material.
you are made up of the fabric
of the universe – threaded
with the very dust of the stars.
know it.
accept it.
and allow it to shine forth

the dance of the wylde

she danced the dance
of the daring and the trusting ~
and to her delight...
magic showed up!

turning

she turned towards the trust
and stopped running.

stretching my soul

i want to stretch my soul way past anything
i've ever known.
i want to push my boundaries over the edge
and lose them forever.
i want to throw the limits away,
watching them shatter to dust.
i want to hold the darkness with ease
knowing it's an integral part of the light.
i want to fill with the calm knowing of trust,
and i want to love all the way to beyond.

the pain

the pain had stopped her too many times.
taking the form of fear,
it gripped her tight.
but now, her belief became more important
than her pain.
turning towards it,
she allowed it to fill her.

me, myself

i commit to me, myself, today.
i vow to listen to and follow and believe
in my goodness.
to recognize my strength
and wield it with the added power of compassion.
to know my heart and trust it
and not turn to outside expectations to feed it,
but rather turn to my own inner guidance
to lead me.
to know that i am the person i want to be
and work to uncover more of my beauty daily.
and to be gentle with myself when
i slip - loving myself even in the darkness.
to me, myself, i give my love.
and it is from me, myself, my love is returned.

giving to us all

in giving them a piece of himself,
mixed with his thoughtfulness,
he gave to us all.

knowing

maybe it's not about the darkness.
and maybe it's not about the light.
maybe it's about the knowing.
the knowing there is sacred always.
even when you can't see it.
maybe it's the knowing that's the
holy part.

maybe it's time

maybe it's time to take care of yourself.
maybe it's time to scream out loud
that you don't have the answers
and you just plain can't figure out what
it's all about...
but you're in this for the full ride.
maybe it's time to stop doin' the half ride.
maybe it's time to step into it all.
to weep your guts out.
to hurt all the way to your core.
to allow that hurt to be there.
maybe it's time to embrace the love
and believe in it even tho it's not always perfect...
but it is always right.
maybe it's time to shout out to your depths
that you do matter
and you will do all in your power to live healthy.
maybe it's time to stop just getting thru,
just surviving.
maybe it's time to grab the gift you've been given
and celebrate every single piece of it -
including the pain that brought you here.
maybe it's time.

the limits

throwing the limits away,
she watched them shatter to dust

slam

slam the door,
i'll open a window.
close my window,
i'll find a crack in the wall.
caulk the opening in the wall,
i'll bust thru the bricks –
because i'm not a victim anymore

new day

she looked out at her new day ~
and believed again.

souls

she didn't just survive -
she became.

her offering

unwrapping her hands
from around her heart,
she offered her all.

i matter

it was when she first dared to see
her truth, that the winds howled.
after a time, it strengthened her
and she spoke her truth
and the earth shook.
and when finally,
she believed her truth –
the stars rejoiced,
the universe opened,
and even her bones sang her song:
"I Matter!"

honor yourself

terri didn't know she was a writer, didn't know she was an artist, she just plain ol' didn't know a heck of a lot of anything. and then some good ol' fashioned, gut wrenching, heart ripping pain gripped her life, and she started to discover things about herself.

she began her journey inward. when the pain got to be too much for her, she spilled out her feelings on paper. wanting to honor those feelings somehow, she added art to them. it was with that mixing of spilling and honoring that bone sighs were born.

needing to find a way to support herself and her sons, she began peddling her watercolor bone sighs shop to shop. thru an amazing journey of tears, miracles, trust, terror, laughter, squeezing her eyes closed tight, and following her heart, somehow bone sigh arts became a real business.

home made books were offered for awhile among her prints and cards. cumbersome to make and lacking the desired quality, there came a time when the books needed to become "real." grabbing her sons, terri and the guys decided to go into print!

without terri's sons, bone sigh arts/books would never ever have become what it has. funny how the very reason for the business became what made the business successful. those boys are everything to both terri and bone sighs!

josh is the oldest. an old soul musician, born entertainer, and a loveable guy! yo yo is their gentle giant who's turning into the world's best graphic designer! and zakk is the logical one. computer geek and mad inventor with the marshmallow heart.

and! the boys have expanded into beginning their own businesses for themselves! (check out the information page for a listing of their websites!)

it's been quite a journey for them all.

terri's still scratchin' her head wonderin' if she'll ever figure any of it out! probably not....but she'll keep trying anyway!

- *info* -

terri st.cloud
15809 menk rd
accokeek md 20607
granolastew@gmail.com

bone sigh arts
BoneSighArts.com

bone sigh books
BoneSighBooks.com

Zakk and Yo's business
Mazuzu.com

Yohan's business
BFG-Productions.com

Josh's business
Poodleman.com

Printed in the United States
203400BV00009B/1-24/P